A marketing & communication blueprint for companies with a cause

MARKETING
ISN'T ABOUT
~~YOU~~

THE TWO THINGS THAT MATTER IF
YOU SELL THINGS THAT MATTER

Adam Fairhead

MARKETING ISN'T ABOUT YOU

The two things that matter if you
sell things that matter

ADAM G FAIRHEAD

About the book

Are you a difference maker? If you answered yes, then you're in luck!

The market is bending increasingly toward you. Buyers increasingly want to support businesses with a cause – businesses just like yours.

Most marketing advice is built for a world we're fast leaving behind. This book addresses the new model, providing a blueprint for a new way to communicate.

About the team

I founded the Fairhead Group with a mission to help difference makers make a difference.

We search for – and find – the best strategies from the world's best thinkers and doers across many different industries and disciplines. Then we distill the best strategies into effective, refined, transformational products. Products that remove the guesswork and risk that are designed exclusively for difference makers, just like you.

Cover page

Introduction

What You'll Get Out Of This

Part One: Attract Your Best Customers

Part Two: Master Your Message

Mission Narrative System (For People Who Don't Know You)

Toolkit

CHAPTER 1

Introduction

Why did I write this book?

Marketing advice as it stands right now, in the overwhelming majority of cases for businesses like yours, is out of date. Consumers have access to more information than ever before and have a zero-tolerance outlook on 'salesy' messaging.

Marketing advice is particularly outdated for companies doing work that matters, where the rules are slightly different.

There's a shift happening. The rules are changing. A friend at Mozilla said it this way, *"People are becoming increasingly intolerant to business without cause."*

The goal of this book is to help business owners learn how to successfully navigate the new world of business by providing guidelines and road maps to the new rules.

What do the new rules mean?

It means companies like yours have a unique advantage the rest of the market doesn't. Here it is:

People want what they've bought – and why they bought it – to mean something bigger for their community, their market, or their industry.

Brendon Burchard, the New York Times Best Seller and motivational coach notes that, *"we've moved away from a pain-oriented society into an aspirational society. Our job is to find the ambition of the people and to touch on that in an authentic and passionate way".*

This is the world we're moving into. Most marketing isn't set up or built for sharing a purpose and direction with readers. *It misses the point.*

Not missing the point

When we think of marketing, we think of a box of tricks designed to get people to do things they may not want to do (but you'd like them to).

We think of free PDFs that promise the world but deliver little more than a sales pitch. We think of banner ads that follow you around for products you don't want (or you'd have bought it already, right?).

This book covers techniques, practices, and methodologies to create a sense of *support and care* between your company and your audience. It's designed to make your chosen audience *want* to hear from you because they know that *you're listening to them, too.* That you understand them, their pains, dreams, hopes, desires, and needs. That you can move their aspirations forward, and that you've already begun doing so.

That connection is a fantastic feeling, and it's precisely the kind of result we'll create for your audience using the contents of this book.

A higher standard

When you share a cause with your audience as a for-profit, nonprofit, or mission-led team of any kind, you have a greater responsibility than a typical organization and your business is held to a higher standard.

A typical organization is responsible to stakeholders, shareholders, and customers. Companies like yours are also responsible for those they're in business to serve on the back-end. Be it a "give back" program, a charity you support, or a difference to make in your community, marketplace, or industry, you're responsible for its success, too.

You need to play a bigger game to achieve that success. You're responsible for making the best products in the world. Placing 3rd lets the mission down. Your marketing must be ethically stronger and strategically more performant than what the market has seen before.

We call it *Meaningful Marketing*. It's what leading difference makers do. And when you're done with this book, it's what you will be equipped to do, too.

Floppy disks and glam rock

I have always been fascinated by great design. How it invokes emotion, how it commands a premium, how it stands the test of time.

In everything I've designed, the Message was important to me, despite not always realizing it.

I remember when I would design and sell floppy disk computer games in the school yard for £3 a copy. Each game needed a story. There were stories about little dragons that could fly and swim. Stories about why zombies were attacking a small town. Stories about why guys in 70's glam rock outfits were racing around on hover boards (I have no idea how I explained that one). They all needed box art and descriptions about what made each game worthy of someone's lunch money.

And they all needed to be made for a particular demographic. The shooter fans had the zombie games. The racer fans were stuck with the 70's glam rock guys. Each game was made with a *Person* in mind, with a *Message* to resonate with each *Person*.

I had no idea I was practicing *Meaningful Marketing* at the time.

Struggling with stories

I'm not really very good at telling stories.

But I've read enough books and watched our Creative team transform enough companies to be intimately familiar with the power of stories.

Stories that aren't necessarily about little white rabbits, magic beans, or having the reader "become the hero", but ones that simply share a journey with somebody.

It turns out that simple ingredients such as empathy, understanding, and caring where someone wants to go are exceptionally powerful tools.

Included in this book is the blueprint our Creative team uses to tell those stories.

"We must establish where [our audience is], where they want to be, what the gap is, what that feels like, not just intellectually, then have them move them to the next stage."

– TONY ROBBINS, INTERNATIONAL PERFORMANCE COACH

The journey ahead

Most of our experiences with marketing don't feel like 'journeys'. They often feel more like roadblocks set up by companies trying to intercept us.

These roadblocks don't speak to what makes *us* special, what sets *us* apart, or what makes *us* unique. Although the organizations behind the barricades are quite happy to coerce us into believing what makes *them* special, what sets *them* apart, and what makes *them* unique.

Our journey has enough challenges, fears and dreams, without concerning ourselves with forced detours.

But if those businesses could accompany us on our journey – maybe even offering to carry a bag or two – we've got the whole journey ahead to hear their message.

We call these journeys 'narratives', and they want to tell themselves...they just need the right structure to do so.

"People don't think in terms of information. They think in terms of narratives. But while people focus on the story itself, information comes along for the ride."

– JONAH BERGER, NYTIMES BEST-SELLER IN MARKETING

CHAPTER 2

What You'll Get Out Of This

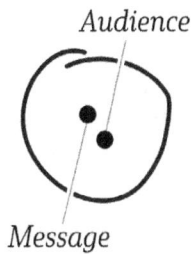

Audience

Message

Here's the thing

The world changed. Marketing didn't.

There are no more mass markets. Consumers want to support businesses with a cause. Marketing 'maps' weren't drawn for businesses with a cause. This one was. I call it *Meaningful Marketing*. Really, it's all that matters for companies that matter.

Over the last few years, our Creative team has tested the idea that **effective online communication comes down to a *Person* and a *Message*. Everything else is just a distraction.** This has turned out to be completely true.

Don't forget to focus on the *Person*. Put the consumer first. Empathize more with them. Love them first, ask questions later. Give them something to be a part of that is bigger than themselves. Make the interaction meaningful for both you and them.

Drawing your ideas

Does your idea make sense? Draw it for me. I drew this book's entire premise on the previous page.

If an idea is simple, we can draw it simply: When pressed to draw our ideas, we might find we fill half a sheet of paper to fully articulate our new idea. This just means we don't understand it well enough, yet.

We like to hide behind complexity: It's easy to make an idea seem complicated, because complications let us hide our lack of clarity from ourselves. Gaining clarity is much harder. Yet it's where everything else comes from.

Understand your concept enough to simplify it into one (or two) sentences: "Create a rocket that deploys from a plane and re-enters orbit in one piece without waste." That's Virgin Galactic's simplified concept. Or, "Good online communication focuses on a *Person* and a *Message*, everything else is a distraction". That concept is the premise behind this book. My drawing provided the clarity that enabled this book to flow easily with high-quality, no-fluff content. The clarity that comes from simplifying your ideas into one drawing or sentence will make it easier for you to put these ideas into motion, just like it did for me.

What you'll learn in this book

There are two big takeaways for you in this book.

The **first** takeaway is how you will identify, engage, and communicate with your target audience (your *Person*) from now on. You will be clearer on who those people are, and how to get them to take action with you.

The **second** takeaway is how to use the narrative structure our Creative team has developed to successfully create meaningful messaging (your *Message*) for your audience to see every time they interact with your company.

Your narrative will be designed to be digestible to both newcomers (prospects) and familiar faces (clients), creating interest and advocacy respectively.

By the end of this book, you will know the right things to say and the order to say them in so that your target audience will raise their hands and say "yes, *this is exactly what I'm looking for. I believe what you believe. Let's talk*".

"If you don't learn how to tell your story, you're not going to grow. Storytelling is the number one way to build your brand."

– DAVE ASPREY, FOUNDER OF BULLETPROOF COFFEE

Consistency is king

Imagine you could turn on a faucet and out flowed your company's ideal prospective customers. Imagine turning it on *right now*. Now, *what do you say to these people?*

If you're like most business owners, you have a vague idea, but you'll hesitate, wondering if you're saying the right things.

Justifiably so: you know that if you say the wrong things, you'll miss an opportunity to make a great impression.

They may interpret your words as a marginalized, self-centered pitch and walk the other way.

Once you know the right things to say, you can say those things every single time. You will know that you can consistently engage prospective customers *every time you turn on that faucet.*

Without knowing the right things to say, and without saying them *consistently*, that faucet is useless to us.

In a later section we will explore what to say and how to say it to your target audience so you can convey your company and message to them in a way they understand every time. It was the same for us, too.

When our first team started out in the marketplace, we decided we would only implement for others what we knew to work reliably for ourselves and for each market we communicated with.

Before we entered the marketplace, we wasted a lot of time experimenting with different channels, tactics and techniques. Finally, we realized it wasn't the channels themselves that were "good" or "bad".

It wasn't until we realized that our performance across every channel was the same that we started to question the way we were communicating. We questioned the best practices and resolved to find "what actually works".

At the time, every client was a happy client, yet new prospects weren't able to grasp what existing clients had grasped. *The two principles that made all the difference were the Person and Message, as we will cover in this book.*

Now, the journey towards focusing on the *Person* and Message is one that our Creative Team watches clients experience on a daily basis. Our Creative Team sees the frustration of things "not working" for their clients. They see the client's reluctance to "relinquish the spotlight" by instead putting it on their prospects. They see the client's leap into empathic, story-driven, personal language for a very specific target audience. And finally, they watch as the clients come to the "oh snap, why didn't we do this sooner" realization that follows.

Empathy isn't what you thought

When you think about it, "putting yourself in other people's shoes" isn't really empathy at all:

Us in their shoes isn't them. It's just us, in their shoes. We're merely imagining ourselves in a different situation.

Imposing our reality on others isn't fair. How can it be empathy if we're still impressing our version of reality onto them?

It takes all kinds of people. Part of humanity's beauty is the diversity of perspective and opinion, but that diversity gets lost in this false kind of "empathy".

Let's not "treat others like we'd like to be treated". Instead, let's treat them like **they'd** like to be treated.

The exercises in *Meaningful Marketing* will challenge us to identify how our target audience would like to be treated.

Online advertising is broken

We don't like being harassed, spammed, or tracked online. Yet we enjoy having more followers and creating bulging social timelines.

What's the difference?

We share our secrets with those we trust. I don't mind friends and family knowing where I am. This information is freely given to those we trust, but we rightly resent it being taken or bartered away from us.

Friends and family don't 'cash in' our trust. I've received emails that literally said, "I saw you on my website today and...". That's just being creepy. Unwanted ads and unwanted emails take advantage of our trust.

Connecting with people and sharing information is what the Internet is all about. But it's about freedom, too. We're smart enough to connect and share with people we trust. We'd never stalk or barter for private information in real life. Why should online be any different?

Meaningful Marketing spends no time on marketing hacks. Instead, we're going to focus on *people*.

How brave are you?

Most teams wouldn't doubt their answer to this question until asked to give away their trade secrets. That which they believe makes them competitive, or unique.

If you could give away your secrets, would you? For example:

Your team's secret sauce: Giving it away means it's no longer secret. It also means your genius is finally, truly on display for others to make a remark about.

How you cut costs or double value: Giving it away means others can do it too. It also means your distinction is easily and favorably compatible to the marketplace.

How you systemize transformation: Giving it away means others can do it too. It also means your audience is better informed and feels safer in your care.

Giving your secrets away means others can do what you do, too. "Others" includes your target audience. Doing so is an opportunity to serve them more fully.

Are you brave enough?

Questions need decisions

Sometimes I can't decide.

Sometimes, both ideas are good, and there's insufficient data to reveal a clear winner.

That's fine. We can test them. In those times, we can put both ideas out into the world, quickly. Show each idea to separate people and see how they respond. Which received better responses?

Get out of your head. If we were going to decide, we would have by now. Getting new eyes and perspectives on the question you have might give you the insight you need to make the call.

Just pick one. If the above fails you, just pick one. They're both as good as each other, so it doesn't really matter. Just make the call and move on.

So, what's it going to be?

Question time

I've prepared three questions, a toolkit, and a challenge.

Neither of us want this to be another book that gets read, enjoyed, and placed on the shelf without implementation. You probably have lots of books doing that job already.

I'm challenging you to do things differently with this one.

After all, you're not an information hoarder (right?) and this isn't intellectual entertainment.

These **questions** (on page 35) will set your intentions as we journey through this book. The **toolkit** (on page 187) will equip you to make those intentions happen. The **challenge** will be your accountability: I want you to prove to me that you'll take action on the contents of this book *within the month.*

Since your company is doing meaningful work, you should be held to a higher standard than the rest. That's why I wrote this book, and why you're reading it.

1. Accountability

At the end of this book, there's going to be a link for you to put your email address in. Once you do, we've prepared a system to keep you accountable for taking action. You'll get progress check-ins for you to reply to, plus reminders and pointers based on the things you learned in this book so that it doesn't "fall off the shelf".

This is an important step.

Without something to hold us accountable, we're far less likely to take action. What we learn risks staying in "good idea" territory, rather than becoming a cornerstone of our companies.

If you don't plan on completing this step, consider *putting the book down* until you're ready to commit to taking action. This book is a *blueprint*; if you don't create what's on it, why study it?

If you do plan on completing this step—to make your marketing memorable, engaging, conversion-oriented, and impactful in your community or cause—then *read on!*

2. Toolkit

Included with the accountability material is a toolkit (page 187).

This is a members-only area where you can access supporting assets – such as worksheets and videos – designed to help you maximize this opportunity.

The toolkit is complimentary with this book.

Since the book was designed to help you create momentum as a meaningful company, it's *my responsibility* as the author to ensure you have what you need to make that happen.

If the book receives updates in the future, you'll have the ability to download revised copies from the toolkit, too.

Our Creative team will continue to add resources to this toolkit over time and send them to you as they are released.

3. Three Questions

Before we move on, answer the three quick questions below. I find if things aren't written down, they don't really count because I'll forget about them. Consider these affirmations to yourself:

Question one: What is your *primary motivation* for reading this book?

....

....

....

Question two: What are you hoping to *learn* as you work your way through this book?

....

....

....

Question three: What will you *do* with your learning once you've finished reading this book?

....

....

....

CHAPTER 3

Part One: Attract Your Best Customers

Why this step exists

I find that most companies think they have this section all figured out already.

Then they go through this exercise and realize how vague their definition of their target audience really was.

You lead a purpose-driven company. There's a reason for that and that reason is bigger than you, or the Profile and Loss sheet.

Whether you're networking, pitching, presenting, selling, or being introduced, if you're talking to the wrong people, you're wasting your time.

Step one is to become clear about who the *right people* are. This is called the "*Attract Your Best Customers*" step, and it's designed to ensure you don't waste any more time.

If you'd like to download the worksheet that goes with this step, go to *fairhead.net/miay*.

"The most important thing to remember is you must know your audience."

– LEWIS HOWES, AUTHOR & FORMER FOOTBALL PLAYER

"It's like you know me better than I do"

When our audience can say *that*, we're already half way towards communicating with the clarity we need to enroll and serve more people more effectively. I heard this quote while sitting in on an ImpactCoaching call between our Creative team and a client.

They hadn't yet made a single observation: they simply cared enough to ask good questions and empathize with the answers that followed.

No fancy language required: there's no "secret marketing hack" that competes with caring enough about the person speaking. Like our grandmothers would say, *"God gave us one mouth and two ears."*

Foundation for every great message: Can a great message that doesn't intimately understand who it was written for actually be great?

The Internet is full of "secret marketing hacks". If you like intellectual entertainment, pick one. They're a hoot.

But when our audience can say *"It's like you know me better than I do"*, we're already half way to our goal of serving people more effectively.

1. Sources

When looking for the data needed to make informed decisions, we tend to over-complicate things.

We likely already have the information we need about our audience, it just happens to be a tangled mess in our minds with distracting tangents protruding from every facet.

We need a way to make sense of it all.

Making sense of the information we already know creates order out of the chaos, aligns our thinking, and makes these facts actionable. The following process will help us put everything in order.

In this section, we're going to comb through what we already know about those we work with, with whom we'd love to work, who we lost along the way, what their pains are, and when they need relief. This will provide you with a clear outline of your target audience (your *Person*). There is space on page 51 to enter your responses to the questions you'll be asked in this section.

Who do you love working with now?

The individuals and companies you think of when you ask yourself this question are important. These people can tell you why they chose to work with you, and they can act as clues as to who your current target audience might be.

We love working with – and serving – those who love working with us because it maximizes the enjoyment on both sides.

We love working with those for whom we can create the greatest outcomes while exerting the least amount of effort. This way we get the maximum return for our effort.

These people are well-equipped to benefit from our genius and we know who they are without thinking too hard. We don't need months of data analysis to reveal their names. Note them down, these are your champions.

Who would you love to work with in the future?

If we don't know where we want to go or who we want to work with, how can we be sure we'll ever get there?

Knowing where we're going enables us to align our efforts and increases the chances that we will arrive where we want to be.

As Craig Groeschel, pastor and best-selling author, knowingly stated, "everyone ends up somewhere. Few people end up there on purpose". This is where vision counts. We want to be able to say: "We've never been there before, and we can't be sure we'll ever get there. But that's where we're going. Who's in?" We might not know if our goal is attainable, but we can make it our purpose to try to reach it.

By leveraging the *Meaningful Marketing* language and communication techniques outlined in this book, we can work with anyone we want.

The people you want to work with in the future are likely people you've never worked with before. They may be out of reach for you at the moment, but everyone works with someone, and that someone can be you. Note these people down, they are your unicorns.

Who did you love working with in the past?

The past leaves us clues about where we're going and how we can influence our future.

Bad gigs show us what to avoid.

Mistakes show us where to improve.

These missteps can teach us as much about where to focus our attention as our successes can.

In this section we're recalling people or organizations that we really enjoyed working with but don't work with anymore, whether it's because they bought our product and that was it, or because things went south so they cancelled. Making a list of these people shows you two things:

First, it presents those who have come through as happy customers who may perhaps engage you again one day.

Second, it reveals those you have let down who may have still been good candidates if you had fixed the areas of service that ultimately turned them away.

Where are the people you love working with located?

Do you know where their world is? What it looks like? What it feels like to live there?

Our environment and its culture shapes us as people, and where our *Person* lives tells us a lot about them.

Remember, buying decisions happen in their world, not yours. The better we know their world, the better equipped we will be to enter it and talk in ways they will understand.

When we examine where the people we love working with live, we have to resist the temptation to say, "They're everywhere! We can help them wherever they are." While noble, that mindset is a disservice to you and to them. They're not everywhere, you just haven't yet named the land.

Are they a native, rural, midwestern dweller? Are they an urban transplant in a major coastal city? Defining where they are and why they are there gives us an insight into their personality and how it influences their objectives (which we will examine in the next chapter).

A key benefit of defining your clients (your *Person*) comes in the form of target advertising. By embracing their culture and showing up in their hometowns, in their magazines, or in their Facebook feeds, we can communicate intimately and intentionally with those we wish to serve.

Where is your *Person* located? Note each place down, these are your new favorite places.

"Don't find customers for your products. Find products for your customers."

– SETH GODIN

What are their pains?

Many companies try to build a product or service, then try to sell it. This is a "solution in search of a problem".

Isn't it better to focus on the people you wish to serve and simply ask them what hurts? This way you'll know what problems exist and can provide direct, relevant solutions.

This simplifies "product development" and "sales" into simply "offering to bring relief those who need it".

Your *Person* will tell you everything you need to know about their pains. All you need to do is ask, listen, and solve them.

You'll be tempted to quantify their pains in relation to your existing products and services. Don't do that. It weakens the clarity of communication we're working toward in this book.

Remember, "offering to bring relief to those who need it" is all about them. Not you.

What are their pains? Note them down in language they would use. These are your new pains, and the ones for which you will create solutions.

When do they need relief?

We behave differently when something is urgent compared to when it's merely "coming up".

If something is urgent, it needs to be dealt with quickly and the situation almost has a sense of borderline desperation. However, if something is coming up in the future, there is some anxiety related to the situation and the potential for analysis paralysis. One risks receiving an overly-emotional response, while the other risks enabling us to become overly-pragmatic.

Being able to empathize with the urgency and mental state of those we wish to serve can help us respect and respond to them in a way they'll appreciate.

For instance, a pressing scenario won't respond well to 35-day turnaround times, and a distant scenario won't respond to next day delivery.

When do they need relief? Note it down; this is your new timeline.

Bringing it all together

We often feel as though we need more information before we're able to make a decision. We want more research, or another blog post, or more YouTube videos to help us get where we need to go. This is called 'stalling'.

We have the information we need. We have identified our *Person*, where they are located, and how we can help them.

At this stage, it's time to stop collecting information. No new data allowed.

But shouldn't it be more complicated? Shouldn't we have graphs and studies and reports? If we maintained a "solution in search of a problem" strategy, it would be more complicated. But serving people who we know need our help doesn't need to be over-thought.

It's time to start working with the data we have. It's in the execution of our data – not the collection – that we uncover the discoveries we've been looking for.

Your answers

Who do you love working with now?

....

....

Who would you love to work with in the future?

....

....

Who did you love working with in the past?

....

....

Where are the people you love working with located?

....

....

What are their pains?

....

....

When do they need a solution?

....

....

2. Objectives

"Genchi genbutsu" is a Japanese phrase that means "going to the source".

Taichii Ohno, former VP of Toyota, supposed that "the root cause of any problem is the key to a lasting solution".

When we look at the pains of our target audience, genchi genbutsu puts our theories of how to solve them to the test.

In this section, we are going to look at an example on page 53 of genchi genbutsu, so that you can note yours down before moving onto the next section.

Notice how asking the question *"Why does this matter?"* enough times will reveal the source objective we're looking for.

What's your source? Note it down, this is your new objective and focus. There is space at the end of this section on page 55 to record your answers.

Genchi Genbutsu in Action

I want to visit England more often.

Innovation is asking more questions to find the source of this statement. At first it sounds like a travel challenge, but are faster planes and cheaper fares 'innovation'?

Let's ask more questions:

Why visit England more often? Because that's where most of my family lives.

Why does this matter? Because seeing them regularly brings us all joy.

Why does this matter? Because without the family-fueled joy, I feel like something is missing in my life.

With these answers, perhaps virtual or augmented reality social tools might also be solutions to explore. Visiting England more often isn't a travel challenge at all, it's about bringing family closer together.

Innovation is asking more questions – divergent ways of *going to the source*.

Example 2: "Get a coaching call"

In this book's Toolkit (page 187), a complimentary 1-on-1 ImpactCoaching call is offered to owners of this book.

Why does this matter?
Try as we may, our first attempt at all these answers is unlikely to be as comprehensive or sophisticated as it would be if we'd done it a thousand times (like a coach).

Why does this matter?
Deeper, fuller answers can give us a stronger sense of how we can target and attract our very best customers.

Why does this matter?
If we can better attract our very best customers, we can serve more of the right people.

Why does this matter?
We will be able to make a greater impact in the lives of those we wish to serve and transform our businesses for the better in the process.

Genchi genbutsu enables us to speak the right language: saying that we want to "impact the lives of those you wish to serve" is much closer to our desired objective than "get a coaching call" is.

Your answers

What is your objective?

....
....

Why does this matter?

....
....

Why does this matter?

....
....

Why does this matter?

....
....

Why does this matter?

....
....

Why does this matter?

....
....

3. The Circle of Influence

John Neffinger and Matthew Kohut, authors of *"Compelling People"*, advocate the use of a circle, which we're referring to as *The Circle of Influence*.

Draw a circle around their hearts. That circle represents the limits of how far they are prepared to listen. Beyond this circle, they can't hear you. Within it, you have their attention. Our job is to get inside and stay inside.

Everyone around us speaks one of two languages, and to understand how to enter the trust circles of our target audience, we must first examine the languages they speak.

1. **The language of 'warmth'** speakers may be untrusting or wary of your intentions. These people want to know that you *understand* them; from comprehension comes **relief and excitement**, and from those emotions comes *an interest in what you have to say.*
   Stephen Fry, English actor and activist, says he sees a color in his mind whenever he hears a note. He 'hears in color'. This kind of emotive language is typical of the language of 'warmth'.

2. **The language of 'strength'** speakers may be tired of time-wasters who don't keep their word. These people want to know you deliver, consistently. From **trust comes respect**, and from respect comes *an interest in what have you say.*

   Gary Vaynerchuk and Seth Godin, both American entrepreneurs, regularly cite a special kind of respect for people who commit to showing up every day in their workplace for long periods of time. This type of appreciation is typical of the language of 'strength'.

We are never told which of these languages we need to speak to which people. *The trick is uncovering which one we need to use with which people.* We figure this out by talking to enough of the people we wish to serve. Being 'bilingual' enables us to create **relief and excitement**, as well as **trust and respect,** and helps us to enter our audience's Circle of Influence so we can serve them better.

Being outside the circle

We all start outside the circle, and consumers have a set of stereotypes for different types of people they consider to be "outside the circle".

For instance, there are a number of "outsider" traits that organizations and individuals notice:

- "They are selling web marketing 'things'. Can't be trusted."
- "Not sure how they come up with those prices."
- "They promise the world and deliver almost nothing."
- "They don't really know if their own stuff works. It's unproven, or they'd be doing a lot better themselves!"

These are – quite rightly – how consumers look at the marketing industry. These points are all valid. We have noticed them, too. To enter their circle, you need to stand out from the rest of the marketing world.

Going inside the circle

Now that we know what we're up against in the eyes of our audience, we know where we are starting our journey from. Here's how we are going to journey from outside to inside.

Our approach will depend on which of the two languages our audience speaks: warmth, or strength.

If empathizing from warmth:

- "It can be frustrating trying to get the web content set up right."

- "It can feel confusing to know which marketing technique is right."

- "It feels scary; making the wrong choice will be costly."

If stating from strength:

- "There's a lot of junky marketing out there."

- "You're right to not trust web marketers; most are liars."

- "They promise the world and usually deliver nothing."

We're saying the same things in each case, while speaking in a language they'll understand.

Being inside the circle

This is where we want to be and stay.

Inside the circle we will have their attention, their trust, and the benefit of the doubt. Here we can see an example of how we'd all like our clients to feel when we're in their circle:

Empathizing from warmth:

- "It's a relief to feel looked after by those who care."

- "It's exciting to know my marketing is taken care of."

Stating from strength:

- "It's empowering to see this being taken care of."

- "Results are consistent; I don't need an alternative."

Another aspect we need to consider is the "register" in which we speak, which goes deeper than warmth and strength. Our register is a reflection of our personality, mindset, beliefs, culture, and interests.

For example, US English is a mutually understood selection of words and phrases, but our urban transplant example from earlier in Part 3 (see page 46) may speak

"US, white-collar professional, optimistic, diplomatic English".

The register our *Person* uses tells us even more about their language and how we might go about speaking the same language as them. When we speak the same language as our *Person*, their trust in us increases.

And trust is precious. This is an asset that all of us should treat with more respect than the revenue that may or may not come with it.

It is from this place of trust that our ideas are shared, our products are enjoyed, and their friends are invited.

Kicking others out

Here's a bonus piece: by understanding the parameters of *The Circle of Influence*, we can elect to kick out competitors if they're under-serving or disrespecting those we wish to serve in the market.

Consider how our Creative team might remove competitors if they chose to do so:

Empathizing from warmth:

• "They don't commit to the level care and support that your business deserves."

• "It can feel devastating to watch someone take your hard-earned resources and give nothing in return."

Stating with strength:

• "They have no history of results; they're figuring it out and winging it on your dollar."

• "They are desperate for the work and will promise anything at the expense of delivering consistent results."

These language factors are important in *The Circle of Influence*; that membrane around our hearts we use to protect ourselves from lousy encounters.

Speaking in both strength and warmth–and understanding the various registers in your *Person's* language–will tell you how to negotiate the membrane of your *Person's* circle. It will also help you serve more of the right people while protecting them from the companies who are just going for their wallets.

What is it like outside the circle?

....
....

What warmth language helps us enter the circle?

....
....

What strength language helps us enter the circle?

....
....

What warmth language keeps us in the circle?

....
....

What strength language keeps us in the circle?

....
....

What warmth language kicks others out?

....

What strength language kicks others out?

....

4. The Person

Data about our target audience is only useful when we act upon it.

The danger of collecting information without applying it is that it can become unwieldy and unusable.

In this stage we're going to address *our* Source data through the lens of *their* Objectives to create a simple, single piece of information.

It's called a '*Person*'. The way we approach this notion is a little different to common, clinical, verbose 'Persona Development' strategies.

We are going to specify who the *Person* you're in business to serve is, if they were to be one person. We are going to mold them out of your Source data, and breathe life into them using your Objectives data.

There's no such thing as "many target audiences" anymore. There are only lots and lots of "individuals", and they all make up your *Person*.

Once you know your *Person*, every piece of meaningful marketing you create or use in the future is going to speak specifically to this individual. Your *Person*.

Be assumptive

Being assumptive gets a bad rap.

You may have heard the catchphrase, *"When you 'assume', you make an 'ass' out of 'u' and 'me'"*. That's only when it's not meant for 'u' or 'me'.

Sometimes to not assume is to be impersonal and disconnected, such as when teams communicate with the marketplace.

If you're looking for people who are looking for X, stating *"You are looking for X"* to the marketplace makes some people say *"no"* and others say *"that's me".*

The "no" crowd was never going to respond anyway. They aren't interested in your product; they aren't your potential customers, so "No" is fine from them. But, for people who find your product relevant to them, the answer is a resounding "Yes".

Using an assumptive phrase such as *"You are looking for X"* is useful to identify which people are your potential customers and which aren't.

Sometimes, to assume is to get to the heart of those your message is to serve.

Where is your Person?

A person's location can drastically change their objectives.

For instance: a native, rural, midwestern dweller might be at higher risk of thinking "real men don't need coaching" than an urban transplant. The urban transplant, however, may have a smaller circle of friends and relish the idea of talking something out with a professional.

Do you remember your answer to this question from the Sources chapter? Note this place from your Sources and keep in mind how your *Person's* objective may be affected.

What language do they speak?

We all talk different languages, so it is critical that we don't forget which one our *Person* speaks.

Because language is a reflection of personality, mindset, beliefs, culture, and interests, it also affects our *Person's* objectives and must be taken into consideration when examining our *Person* as a whole.

What's their language? Note this place from your Sources and keep in mind how your *Person's* objective may be affected because of it. This is your language now.

What does your Person do?

For most of us, including our target audience, our work takes up a huge portion of our lives.

But what our job description is and what we call ourselves can be two different things.

What we choose to call ourselves is as important as the role our work represents. Are you an accountant or CFO? A cook or a chef? An intern or an apprentice?
A proprietor or an entrepreneur?

The answer may hint at our job description, but the different titles for the same jobs indicate to your audience how you'd like to be perceived.

Knowing what our *Person* does and which job title they use tells us a lot about their lives, indicates the language they use, and reveals the challenges they face.

What do they do? Note it down, this is your new special interest.

Note: *there are sometimes more than one "Person", so the answers section on page 71 exposes two spaces in case there are two key demographics.*

What does your Person 'like'?

This question refers to Facebook, or Instagram, or whatever primary social network your *Person* belongs to.

'Liking' things may be an arbitrary and haphazard pastime, but it leaves clues.

We all want to be associated with things that we believe express the fabric of who we are, such as the football club we support, or the fact that we're "in business", or our wealth of knowledge about our special interest.

Does your *Person* join non-profit Facebook Groups? Retweet certain activists? 'Like' select business magazine Facebook Pages?

Follow the clues and note them down. These are our new social hangouts.

Your answers (Person A)

They live in...

....

....

Their language is...

....

....

Their age/gender/marital status is...

....

....

Their occupation is...

....

....

The Facebook Pages they like are...

....

....

They dream of...

....

....

Your answers (Person B, optional)

They live in...

....

....

Their language is...

....

....

Their age/gender/marital status is...

....

....

Their occupation is...

....

....

The Facebook Pages they like are...

....

....

They dream of...

....

....

Putting it all together

Everything we just identified about our target audience, from where they live to what they are interested in on social media, makes up our *Person*.

Everybody else is merely a distraction. They can't afford your time or attention anymore. And you can't afford to give it to them.

From now on, the more you serve this *Person*, the more your organization succeeds.

Keep this *Person* written down, close at hand, and think about them often. Dedicate your business to them. Write them letters of advocacy and appreciation. Think about ways you can help them live their best life. Go where they go. Be interested in what they're interested in. Talk their language. Be in their world.

This is the *Meaningful Marketing* way to approach the market. Make yourself meaningful in your *Person's* world and meet them where they are, on their level.

Now that we make great company for them and we know how to access this *Person* on-demand, we need to know what to say. We need to master our message.

CHAPTER 4

Part Two: Master Your Message

Why this step exists

We engage with people (and things) we trust, be it a trusty old car that never lets us down or a trusted friend we can share anything with.

Brené Brown uses the acronym BRAVING to define trust and it breaks down into the following:

- **Boundaries** (having them)
- **Reliability** (being consistently true to your word)
- **Accountability** (owning mistakes and making amends)
- **Vault** (keeping a confidence)
- **Integrity** (choosing courage over comfort)
- **Non-judgement** (we can both struggle and ask for help)
- **Generosity** (assuming best intentions and behaviors)

In the previous chapter we became specific about who we're in business to serve, and in this chapter we're going to learn how to communicate empathically and selflessly enough to build trust and confidence in those same people.

Do your industry's 'walls' work for you?

The way we communicate our *Message* to the *Person* we've decided to serve affects our work deeply.

You see, you're not in the market you think you're in (unless you really want to be in the market you think you're in).

A photographer may think they are in the "photography" market, but is that true? Or, are they in the "making memories" market? Is a restaurant in the "restaurant" business or are they in the "entertain guests for an hour" business?

Do you simply offer a service, or do you do work that matters and is specifically designed resolve problems that your clients face?

The current walls of the industry you're interested in weren't built for you. They are there to tell you how to do your work the same as everyone else and to show your prospects how to judge you.

For example: A photographer takes photos, and their prospective clients know this. Photographers don't offer catering during the shoot so everyone can loosen up and relax over a drink or a snack before the photos. That's not what photographers do. That's not inside the photography industry's walls.

But it could be what a photographer does if someone in that industry decides that the current walls of the photography business don't work for them.

Car brands compete against car brands... despite there being enough cars. Why does Rolls-Royce choose to compete against yachts instead of cars? *Because the walls didn't work for them.*

Restaurants compete on their own menus... despite already having too many options. If they instead remembered that they are in the "entertain for an hour" business, might some of them take a different approach to being a restaurant?

Do the business and marketing walls work for you? What happens if you decide 'No'? The way we communicate our Message is a statement to the market about who we are serving, and how we plan to help them. Our message is bigger than us, and the walls don't matter.

By looking outside the walls of our chosen industry, we change the scope of what we think about. The focus becomes about the visitor and what might make them happier, rather than merely focusing on our own craft.

Bigger than you

It is natural to assume that great communication will focus on clear, empathic, effective ways of articulating yourself.

However, in the *Meaningful Marketing* philosophy, the opposite is true: great communication will focus on clear, empathic, effective ways of articulating *them*.

Messages are processed within the world of our minds. In other words, the best apps understand and fully utilize the operating system for which they're designed.

You belong in the narrative, but only when (and to the degree that) your intentions are clear and trust exists. Since the story is about them (your *Person*), your heart for service from the previous chapter shines through when you offer to help.

Thanks to the mission behind your organization, not only will engaging you seem natural to your *Person*, but it becomes an expression of a shared belief.

This 10-section chapter will affect the ways you communicate with your website, your social media, your networking, your presentations, and beyond.

Now is the best time to fill in the blanks

Sometimes, we're amazed at how time seems to fly by.

Sometimes, we're amazed by what we can do in such a short amount of time.

Which of these feelings do you normally have?

For example, one person could have a concept for a book so they write it and list it on Amazon. They're amazed by how much was done so quickly.

But another person could have a concept for a book so they ponder it, make notes, and wonder what it could be like to be a published author. They're amazed about how time flew by since they wrote down their original idea.

The same applies to the *Meaningful Marketing* questions we're covering in this book; time will amaze us, one way or another.

Which person would you prefer to be?

Mission Narrative System
(For People Who Don't Know You)

Mission Narrative messaging

The *Mission Narrative* is a way to quickly earn the attention and trust of people who don't yet know us.

For years our team tried to figure out "what truly matters" – the things that actually make a difference when it comes to selling online. We tried the "tricks", tried the "courses", and searched for the nuggets that would make a difference when combined.

It was only when we found the best pieces from the best minds then brought them all together that we were able to create predictable increases in enrollment, engagement, and sales for our business. We attribute these pieces to Mission Narratives.

People don't normally have business problems, they have communication problems that affect their business. Most people try to start a business by focusing on their product or service and how great it is. When they experience low sales, they think there must be something wrong with their product or service. In reality, this rarely the case. It is more likely that they are experiencing issues in the way they communicate their product to their audience.

That's where the Mission Narrative comes in.

Why this step exists

There are three key reasons for why the Mission Narrative is able to perform as well as it does:

Teams need to win people over to their ideas. If they can't do that, their ideas are non-starters and their businesses don't grow. In all stages of development, companies and teams doing meaningful work need to articulate their value to an unconvinced audience.

People respond best to empathy. Susan Scott cites in her book *Fierce Conversations* that *"understanding is more important than love"*. Showing understanding is at the core of the Mission Narrative structure and it wins people over. Our *Person* doesn't need more features or rebuttals. They don't need to be patronized as a 'hero' of our story. They need to feel that someone truly cares enough to support them through the journey they are taking.

The best teams have a mission. Seth Godin cites in his book *Tribes* that *"The secret of leadership is simple: Do what you believe in. Paint a picture of the future. Go there."* The mission behind your company is not just an internal factor but an opportunity to create engagement with your audience as an expression of a shared belief.

The following points will help you create an empathetic message that also showcases your mission to win over your audience.

1. Pattern interrupt

Imagine the Star Wars books had printed on the cover, "*Vader is Luke's Dad, Empire Gets Defeated, Merchandise Now Available*". Would you read the book?

What if it said, "*We can't trust the Empire any longer. Luke has had enough: It's time to make a change*". Perhaps this is a little more relatable with many of today's audiences.

The best covers grab you with a statement or question that you've already been pondering. Again, it's not about your company or team, it's about your *Person*, your audience.

We begin our message with a gift: **the comfort your *Person* finds in knowing they're not about to be sold to.**

Instead, you understand the statement or question they've been pondering.

Your goal is to show your *Person* that your message and business are about them. Interrupt the marketing pattern that other companies have laid out and focus on your audience immediately.

Example 1: "Prospects don't know your unique value."

This is how we open one of our Creative team's messages on the BuiltForImpact.net website.

We feature a Siamese Fighting Fish – a beautiful, unique creature – swimming into view at the top of the page, with this statement in place.

Below the headline it says, "*Discover how to captivate visitors on your website – and get them to take action.*"

Compared to the Business-to-Business (B2B) product or service sites you may have experienced in the past, our Creative team hasn't once mentioned what they do. There's no "*innovative B2B solutions*", "*we offer*", or similar esoteric, self-serving language to be found anywhere in sight.

Our team may not be right for that visitor. Then again, they might be. We'll never know until we build trust outside of any expectation of an engagement. This is a Pattern Interrupt.

Example 2: "Tap on your investment."

This is relatable to ethnic-minority business owners who have ever sought investment.

In this example, we see an image of investment money with the headline, *"Tap on your investment"*.

When the visitor moves their cursor to the investment money, it jumps to another location on the screen. Over and over. The headline becomes *"Difficult, isn't it? It doesn't have to be..."*

The page proceeds to empathize with the challenge of minority entrepreneurs, then connects them with free resources and bootcamps to help rectify the problem.

The gift disarms visitors from the feeling they may be peddled a product at any moment. Your message begins with a focus on your audience and where they are right now.

That's a *Pattern Interrupt*.

Pattern Interrupt Idea A

....

....

....

....

Pattern Interrupt Idea B

....

....

....

....

2. A Clarifying, Indoctrinating Description

Ever watched a perfume advertisement?

You never really know what you're watching until the very end, when the ad announces a new fragrance. Until then, you're wondering what on Earth is going on.

Perfume companies seem to get away with it. For the rest of us, we need to be clear and succinct about what we do and how we do it, without selling, early in our communication. Otherwise visitors may quietly ponder, *"Where is this all going?"*

Following the *Pattern Interrupt*, we're going to make our intentions clear for them. The *Pattern Interrupt* disarms buyer defenses and ensures they're prepared to listen. The *Clarifying, Indoctrinating Description* ensures they know that your message is worth listening to.

'What's in the box?' What does your business do? Time to write it down.

Example 1: One-page distillation

"BuiltForImpact is a focused, one-page distillation of your company's message with a deliberate, concentrated focus on ethical and effective lead-generational sales."

BuiltForImpact is a clinical, 'non-salesy' distillation of 'what's in the box'. Your distillation only needs to be between one and three sentences long.

Notice we don't say it's a *"revolutionary, innovative Business-to-Business & Business-to-Consumer solution for transformative digital results"* or something equally esoteric.

Example 2: Virtual receptionist

"We are a boutique virtual receptionist service serving law firms in the United States & Canada. We answer incoming calls, schedule appointments, phone your clients to relay messages, and free up your time so you can work in peace."
– Emily L.

This is a perfect example of a Clarifying, Indoctrinating Description because these two sentences describe what they do, for whom, and to what end. Done. The details can all come later when the reader cares to know more.

Your answers

Your clarifying, indoctrination description includes...

....

....

....

....

....

....

....

....

....

....

3. Proof of Impact

Nobody likes going first.

Whether it's at a conference group activity or a game of charades, 'going first' is always more uncomfortable than taking part in the activity after the rules and rhythms are proven.

When you read the *Clarifying, Indoctrinating Description*, the same rules apply. Readers will likely ask themselves, *"Anybody else think these guys are worth listening to?"*

That's what *Proof of Impact* is for. It moves you from *"listen to me"* to *"listen to the person from whom people just like you get their advice"*. It reassures your readers that someone else has already gone first and the product or service your company offers is tried and true.

Numbers can lie

Numbers and statistics about a company's followers or revenue can be both impressive and deceptive. We need to make sure ours are impressive without deception.

For instance:

Ten thousand followers: But are they engaged? A hundred loyal advocates beat droves of lukewarm followers.

Ten million in revenue: But is it profitable? Twitter was $167 million in the red in 2017. One million and profitable beats ten million and sinking.

Ten new signups: But are any of them getting any value out of what you're making available? Many messages tout empty numbers: one transformation beats 100 failures.

Ten new reviews: But are they positive or negative? Customers tend to trust the neutral/negative ones more. One real, honest review beats ten unbelievable ones.

Example 1: It really works.

"When we tried Fairhead Creative, our conversion doubled: it was the highest [Return on Investment] on anything we ever spent. We became one of the top [...] companies in our niche." – Simon B.

This is an endorsement by one of our Creative team's clients. We made a statement that backed up our Indoctrination Description for that product, which demonstrates to our audience that we really know what we're doing.

Example 2: Those you may recognize.

People are impressed by seeing the logos of major publications on your site, such as the Huffington Post and Inc.com.

But not for the reasons one might think.

The prestige of the brands is overshadowed by the familiarity to your audience. These are publications that our audience is familiar with in their world. You are new to their world, Huffington Post is not. Your placement on that website demonstrates that you are neighbors in the same universe.

We've been published in...

....

....

....

A big win we've celebrated is...

....

....

....

A fantastic review or testimonial we've received is (1)...

....

....

A fantastic review or testimonial we've received is (2)...

....

....

4. Defining the Problem

"Where does it hurt, sir?"

In a doctor's appointment, if I'm handed a bottle of antibiotics before I've even had a chance to explain what my ailments are, I'm going nowhere near those pills.

Half of the doctor's job is to listen and repeat back to the patient what their problem is. If the doctor can define and describe it better than we can ourselves, we know they've "got it".

Knowing the battle is half the battle. And it's the half that most people who don't practice *Meaningful Marketing* seem to forget all about.

In this step, we're going to go through a few questions to be sure we're fully *Defining the Problem* of our *Person*.

1. They wish...

Our *Person* longs for something, be it to gain something or escape something, and there's usually an escape behind most pursuits of gain. So, what's the longing of our *Person*? What do they wish to gain or escape?

2. They fear...

The flip-side of those desired gains or escapes is the results they anticipate if they're unsuccessful. As is the case with fear, it's bigger and scarier than reality. Relating to this warped vision of the future helps them understand that you understand how they feel.

3. They feel...

In light of the desired gain or escape and the fear associated with potentially missing out on these aspirations, what feelings are they experiencing?

Be specific. Beyond sad, do they feel lonely? Guilty? Victimized? Inferior? Beyond afraid, do they feel insecure? Humiliated? Overwhelmed? Reach for deep feeling words. Again, this will help your *Person* understand that you understand them.

4. They don't have...

Every problem brings limitations. A lack of money limits purchasing power. A lack of love limits happiness. A lack of health limits life. What does our *Person* lack as a result of their problem?

5. They can't...

Moving beyond what they don't have, what can't they do as a result of their problem? For instance, if they don't have their health, they can't live their life to the fullest. If they don't have their confidence, they can't have the marriage or career they really want.

6. Therefore...

Wrap it all up: where does this leave our *Person*? All in all, what consequences must our *Person* live with until or unless things change? What do they want?

Your answers

They wish...

....
....

They fear...

....
....

They feel...

....
....

They don't have...

....
....

They can't...

....
....

Therefore...

....
....

5. Defining the Solution

We're in alignment with our *Person* now.

When someone understands our troubles, we assume they also understand where we want to go, perhaps even better than we do. The better we understand our *Person*, the more our *Person* will then trust we know how to make the solution happen.

We're still not going to focus on what value you can bring to them in order to make their problems go away. Instead, we're merely painting a clear picture of what life will look like when the problem has gone away, from the vantage point of the problem.

For instance, from the perspective of someone with health problems, the Solution will look like a life of energy, opportunity, shared experiences, and watching their kids (or grandkids) grow up. Even though we are currently facing the problem, we can see what the situation will look like after a solution is found.

In this step, we're going to go through a few questions to be sure we're fully *Defining the Solution* of our *Person*.

1. They have...

Our *Person* was longing for something, and now they have it. What is 'it'?

For instance, this could be an item, a state of mind, more confidence, an achievement, or an ability they didn't have before.

2. They're free of...

As part of having gained the *Solution* they were looking for, our *Person* is free from the shackles of their problem. What is it they're now free of that they need not put up with, or wrestle with, or fear, or settle for?

3. They feel...

While our *Person* ponders having the *Solution*, what feelings are they experiencing?

Again, be specific. Beyond happy, do they feel proud? Powerful? Liberated? Courageous? Peaceful? Safe? Reach for deep feeling words. Again, this will help your *Person* understand that you understand them.

4. They can...

What can our *Person* do as a result of their *Solution*? How has this life change equipped them to do things they couldn't do before?

It's true that they may not do these things once they have the *Solution*. People tend to romanticize how they think they'll behave, but that's okay. At this stage, we should romanticize with them. It's part of their journey.

5. Therefore...

Wrap it all up: where does this leave our *Person*? What does life moving forward from this place look like for them?

Your answers

They have...

....

....

They're free of...

....

....

They feel...

....

....

They can...

....

....

Therefore...

....

....

6. Show the Product

Let's draw a mental map.

There's Problem Island, and there's Solution Island. Each island is quite small, with a body of water between them.

At this stage, we've painted a picture of both islands, through the eyes of our *Person*. Their question at this stage will be, "*So how do I get there?*"

The answer may be for them to swim in the dangerous waters between these islands, chancing the waves. Or the answer may be for them to fashion a boat out of the local foliage and row themselves across. Or they could just walk across the bridge. *Your product is the bridge.*

In this step we're still not doing any 'selling'. We don't need to; we need only point to the bridge and allow them to cross it if they want to.

By pointing out the water, the boat resources and the bridge, they're smart enough to make their own decision about whether or not the product is a sound option.

Be specific about the form it takes. About how long it takes to complete, or assemble, or arrive. About the price, about how to get started.

What is the product?

....

....

What are the dimensions/specifics?

....

....

How long does it take to complete, assemble, or arrive?

....

....

How much does it cost?

....

....

What does it look like? Feel like? How can we show this?

....

....

Best in the world

If your Product was the best in the world in your field, how would you behave differently?

Would you offer greater guarantees? With the confidence of being the best, would your guarantees become stronger?

Would your service become more selective? With an abundance of prospects, would you accept the same customers or clients?

Would you behave differently? With no superiors, are there activities, behaviors, or tolerances you'd change?

Are there features you would cut? With the title of 'best', would you choose to focus more exclusively on your best works?

These are things that separate where you are now from where you would be if you were the best in the world.

So why not change them now and start closing the gap?

The gift of asking for more

How do you feel about offering your Product, and asking for more?

"Buy another." Because it's good for you, and you should do it again. To not encourage you to is to not care at all about your progress.

"Upgrade to this." Because these benefits will help you, and if we didn't let you know that, it would make us an opportunity thief and a bad friend.

"Donate to this cause." Because it is meaningful and significant to you. The biggest and best gift of all: the gift of no personal gain at all, except for the reward you'll feel inside.

Is the story we tell ourselves about our Product one of care and service, or one of scarcity and imposition?

Which is less selfish? Keep this in mind whenever you *Show Your Product.*

7. The Mission

So, you "get it".

You understand the *Person's* journey. Your product fits. The next question is *why you?*

Are you a conglomerate that spotted a market need and filled it, providing support until the experiment ends?

Or are you someone who's been where they've been and has a mission bigger than you or them?

For instance, my teams all exist to help difference makers make a difference and to fund the fight against human trafficking. The mission to love people doing meaningful work means these are products you *want* to buy, not only to solve a problem but as an expression of a shared belief.

The mission of TOMS Shoes is to give a child in need of shoes a pair each time a customer makes a purchase. You buy TOMS because of the shoes and because of what those shoes mean. Their mission becomes your mission, too.

This is the only area of your message in which you're permitted to talk about yourself. So get personal, go deep, and share the mission behind the message.

Your answers

Who founded the organization, and why did they?

....

....

....

How can they relate and/or empathize with the *Person*?

....

....

....

As a result of their empathy, the mission is...

....

....

....

The give-back or impact we create in the world is...

....

....

....

What difference does the *Person's* involvement make?

....

....

....

Embrace your (weird) mission

What is 'weird', anyway?

If you're on a mission to do meaningful, relevant work, the answer might be **you.**

If you're relentlessly pursuing your genius for a cause greater than yourself, the answer might be **you.**

The market is increasingly conscious about the presence or lack of a *Mission*. Most businesses and companies are too afraid to embrace the vulnerability of sharing their *Mission*.

If you're happy with the status quo, with safely stowing yourself away for retirement instead of contributing toward something weird, then **don't worry: you're fine.**

(Or are you?)

8. Easy Enrollment

People don't usually buy right away. And that's fine, we're not really 'selling' right away.

But we do want everybody to take the first step. We want their search for a fix to stop with us.

Making sales requires permission from the *Person*. Equipping our *Person* to take the first step does not. We get to decide if and when we start serving our *Person*. This is our opportunity to serve.

In this step, we're going to define what "impossible to not open" gift we can give our *Person*.

Be generous. More generous than your competitors. More generous than your current idea.

Why does this matter? Because your *Person* has likely seen enough in their time to consider most offers underwhelming. Most offers *are* underwhelming.

To truly stop the search, we need to change the game.

These next few questions will help you pick the right gift for your *Person*.

You have permission to serve your audience

"If only they'd buy, then they'd know how great we are."

You don't want to give away your permission to serve your audience, you want to use it:

You know better: Why wait for those who don't yet believe in your work to give you permission to serve them?

Adopt their risk: Consider the risks others have to take when choosing to work with you. Can you take on that risk yourself?

There are few rules: But there's no rule that says value and transformation can only occur after someone pays for it. You choose your rules.

You've always had – and always will have – permission to serve. Make sure your *Easy Enrollment* offer gives them every reason to say "Yes, we accept your offer to serve us".

The marketplace needs your permission

Now we know we have permission to serve, we can also give permission away.

It's *ours* to give away. But what does "giving permission" mean in the marketplace?

Permission to make the wrong decision. Now they can say 'Yes' to you and risk being wrong (you'll let them know and let them go). Otherwise, they may risk saying 'Yes' to someone else and be stuck with something that's not for them.

Permission to make mistakes. Now they can be guided through their mistakes by you rather than suffering the consequences of their mistakes because they're with someone who cares more about the cheque than helping people.

Permission to be greater than they believed. Now they can make bigger, better decisions because you raised them to new heights instead of letting them limit themselves to marginal, fractional options because no one else told them they're good enough.

You have many types of permission to give to whomever you please. Will you?

1. For the first step, our Person can...

Here, we must decide what that first step looks like. The second step on the bridge is easier for our *Person* to take once they've taken the first.

For instance, a Bed & Breakfast coach may find that the first breakthrough comes once their client hires their first cleaner. So, this first step must make that breakthrough happen. A coach alone may be ignored, but if they provide their prospective *Person* with clear benefits from choosing their company, the guide is more likely to gain that client. For example, the guide could offer to pay the cleaner's first month salary if the arrangement doesn't work out in 28 days, providing the client makes the hire from a certain website within the next 14 days. Benefits such as this will help encourage prospective clients to take the step.

A subscription service may find that the first breakthrough comes once their *Person* uses a particular feature to fruition. So, this step must make that usage happen. A free trial to 'everything' may be too much, but ensuring they succeed in one area may be priceless to the company and client.

Our ImpactCoaching team gives away the worksheets, video training, and a 1-on-1 expert guidance for the entire *Attract Your Best Customers* chapter of the *Meaningful Marketing* process; it only takes 30-45 minutes to complete and it makes a huge difference for our *Person* (that's you!).

2. We make it easy because...

Nobody reads white papers and lengthy free eBooks anymore. They may seem easy, but they're not; they require a *lot* of time to read.

A one-page cheatsheet you can consume in 10 minutes outperforms a 100-page eBook that takes 4 weeks to complete.

A video explaining how to achieve something is easier than scheduling a call because the call requires scheduling, and it also sparks the client's fear or dislike of being pitched a product.

A packet sent in the mail is easier than showing up in person for an event because the packet can be opened in the privacy and social safety of your own home, whereas an event requires getting ready and going there, finding the place, parking, and interacting with the unknown.

Consider how you can make your *Easy Enrollment* piece as radically simple for your *Person* as possible.

3. There's no risk because...

Reverse the risk.

You believe in your ability to serve. They don't. So, take responsibility for the risk until they believe in your ability, too.

If you need someone to get on the phone with you, you could reverse the risk by paying them $200 if they realize the call wasn't valuable to them.

If you need them to pay for something, remove the cost, or give them a full money-back guarantee, so there's a guarantee that they won't be out of pocket.

If you need them to follow your advice, promise something valuable to them if the advice doesn't work, so that there's a guaranteed upside in doing what you say.

Whatever the risk associated with taking the first step with you is, eliminate or reduce it as much as possible for your *Person*. The less risk involved, the more likely they'll take the first step.

And, if your ability to serve is powerful enough, the increase in enrollment will far outpace any conceivable risk or downside associated with the offer you'll make.

4. What happens next is...

If you don't know what's behind a door, you're less likely to open it. This applies to *Easy Enrollment*, too.

When our Creative team creates a website, every form must be very specific about what happens next. Clients can see exactly what the email address will be used for, precisely what they will receive by email and when, what page they will be taken to next... you get the idea.

There's a journey you have prepared for your *Person* to make. *Show them that journey.*

If there's a 14Kb PDF file coming by email, followed by an email checking in with them in 24 hours, say so.

If there's a request for an appointment to schedule a 30-minute phone call with you on the next page, say so.

Be specific. Most of the concern around online enrollment is due to the lack of clarity around the question, *"What will happen if I do this?"*

Your answers

They can...

....

....

....

We make it easy because...

....

....

....

There's no risk because...

....

....

....

What happens next is...

....

....

....

Consider making it clear who your product is not for

But isn't selling about engaging, not preventing?

Not always:

Preventing the wrong decision: denying enrollment to the wrong piece of work shows that you have your prospective clients' best interests at heart, not their email address or their wallet.

Preventing the wrong timing: being on-demand may be convenient, but if it's not right for your *Person*, forgoing it can increase demand.

Preventative selling prevents mistakes, misuse, and dilution.

Ensure your *Easy Enrollment* offer isn't 'enabling' when you should be 'preventing'.

The Lemonade Button

Is engaging with your offer as easy as pushing a button?

Vending machines are clear about what each button gives us. The Lemonade Button is unashamedly Lemonade:

It'll turn many away: We won't push it unless we want lemonade.

Some will surely press: We'll push it if we want lemonade. And we'll be happy with the result.

No guesswork.

The alternative to no guesswork is to be less specific about our Product in an attempt to get our button pushed more often and by those who didn't actually want lemonade. Consequently, it leaves those who wanted lemonade to risk pushing other buttons because they don't know what the result of our button is.

How could your team's work be more confidently clear like The Lemonade Button?

The offer you're afraid to make

You might already know what it is.

It's the one your team may have all thought of but never voiced because it's much too risky.

The riskier it feels, the bigger problem you have:

It feels risky when your work needs work: How sure are you that your team's work will beat expectations? Aggressive guarantees aren't risky if the answer is '99%'.

It feels scary when nobody else does what our company does: They probably don't do it for the same reasons you hesitate – they're afraid of the risk. But that's good: it means you get to go first.

If the consequent challenge is merely to "perfect your work", what's stopping you? Weren't you going to attempt that anyway?

No more 'opt-ins'

"What should I make so that people will buy my thing?"

Our creative team hears this one a lot. When you position your *Easy Enrollment* offer, eschew the oft-touted 'opt-in':

If your product isn't great, a 'twist' won't fix it. Great marketing is great communication. Making your product sound better than it isn't marketing, it's deception.

If your product isn't clear, 'marketing-speak' won't fix it. Great marketing speaks the language of the buyer. If you're trying to sound clever, you're making it worse.

If people won't try it, 'things' won't fix it. Great marketing makes it easy for the right people to start. Offering unrelated 'stuff' instead only delays getting them ready to start.

No more 'opt-ins'; instead, focus on *Easy Enrollment*.

Why not communicate clearly and start helping people move from *Problem* to *Solution*, instead of peppering their inbox with more junk they'll never read? They have enough email junk from other companies. I'm challenging you to be different.

9. Supporting Content

You've made a great *Easy Enrollment* offer that makes "Yes" a hopeful inevitability to hear form your customers.

What if they say "No"?

No message gets a 100% conversion rate. If they're still here but they're saying No, that means your business is either not a fit for them, or that they still have questions.

In the latter case, the *Supporting Content* section is designed to answer those questions. Every remaining question or concern your audience has is material for you to cover. Their concerns are your content strategy.

What are their concerns? Make an article about each one and address it thoroughly. Not as a rebuttal, but as another gift.

What are their questions? Again, make an article about each one. These are opportunities for you to selflessly teach what you know. Give away your secrets.

Few businesses think to address these concerns or dare to give away their secrets. After each piece of content, you can reintroduce your audience and potential clients to your *Easy Enrollment* offer.

Your answers

A concern the *Person* may still have is...

....

....

A concern the *Person* may still have is...

....

....

A question the *Person* may still have is...

....

....

A question the *Person* may still have is...

....

....

A case study of someone who went before them is...

....

....

A case study of someone who went before them is...

....

....

10. Social Share

Seth Godin describes "remarkable" things as "things worth making a remark about".

If your *Person* wants to make a remark about your message, how should they do that?

Buttons that ask you to "Tweet this" and "Like us on Facebook" are so common that we're blind to them.

We can do better. We want to make sure we are creating a way for our *Person* to remark on our products or business without them asking "What would you like me to tweet, and to whom?" or "Where should I share this link, and what should I say about it?"

Providing direction and structure to the social media share turns the action into an intentional activity. For example, "Invite a friend and get $50". Or "1,000 signups this month and we'll give $1,000 to X charity".

There's no harm in adding "share" buttons, but our *Person* is more likely to understand our intentions behind asking them to follow through with the actions we request of them if we can add intention to the share.

Your answers

A way the *Person* can share our business to others is...

....

....

....

A way the *Person* can share our business to others is...

....

....

....

Putting it all together

This is our message, from the Pattern Interrupt to the Social Share and everything we covered in between.

All other statements, elaborations, offers and incentives are distractions. We don't tell those stories anymore.

From now on, the more frequently and more effectively you share this message, the more your organization succeeds.

Keep this message written down, close at hand, and focus your optimizations around refining and perfecting this message rather than coming up with alternatives to distract and dilute your work. Understand your audience's *Problem* more intimately. Make the *Easy Enrollment* step even easier to say "Yes" to. You get the idea.

When our message is this detailed and intentional, we're connecting with our *Person*, empathizing with them, understanding them, and taking the initiative on their behalf. We're lavishing upon them.

This is the *Meaningful Marketing* way to create a message for those we wish to serve.

Shared Heritage System
(For People Who Know You)

Shared Heritage messaging

The *Shared Heritage* is a way to maintain the enrollment, attention, and trust of those who know about us, our ideas, and our work.

The way you speak to strangers is different than how you speak with your friends. The narrative you share changes when the *Person* has an existing relationship with you. This structure of Shared Heritage was created by modeling Apple's development of a fanatical fan base that is ready to buy whatever is released, before they even know what it is.

The Shared Heritage process combines your relationship to your clients with the ongoing development and mutual-advocacy of your company's mission. In *Rework*, Jason Fried and David Heinemeier Hansson state that *"great businesses have a point of view, not just a product of service"*.

We'll cover the key components of *Shared Heritage* in the coming pages.

The 'i' in iPhone

Every year Apple does a keynote, and every year they tell us a story.

Apple uses that story to manufacture the mystique and excitement around their products. Without the story, – the narrative – their keynotes are merely press releases about smartphones with better tech specs.

This is the story they tell us:

Heritage: Here's where we've been, together. We're so proud of how far we've come, aren't you?

Desire: We've created the next step in the journey you're taking. Amazing, isn't it?

Future: Look ahead, here's what our shared future looks like together. It's exciting, isn't it?

It's the story we buy; the heritage, the desire, and the future. And it's the story we experience every time we use their products.

The story is the 'i' in iPhone.

1. The Heritage

When we reminisce about a company, family, or expedition, we're able to recall many things that happened over that time that we may have forgotten about.

In the book Pre-Suasion, Robert Cialdini states, *"The main purpose of speech is to direct listeners' attention to a selected sector of reality"*. If this is the case (which it is), and if we're on a journey with our audience at this stage (which we are), then the most logical view to begin with is the one we have in the rear view mirror.

If we've made progress of late, be it in our professional or personal lives, our pride in our achievements compounds with the focus we give it.

This is why *Shared Heritage* starts by focusing on the heritage we share.

Heritage and homelessness

Imagine you're walking along on a street not far from your home. A homeless person walks up to you and asks for spare change. What do you do?

"I don't know who you are, but here's a dollar." Whether you tell him you don't have any or you hand him a buck, you're unlikely to overthink it or continue to ponder it moments later. The encounter barely registers emotionally or financially.

"You're like me, here's everything I have." What if they told you they're from your hometown, went to the same school as you, moved here and fell upon hard times? Are you going to merely give him your spare change, or are you going to give him shelter, food, council, and support?

You and he are still the same people in both scenarios. All that changed was the knowledge of shared experiences. You realize you're just like him. Despite not sharing the same blood, a shared heritage is enough to make you behave as you do. As teams doing important work in the marketplace, we should think hard about what heritage we share with those we wish to serve. What could it do to the quality of our relationships with them?

Example

In 2018, Apple announced the release of their iPhone Xs and iPhone Xr smartphones, alongside a milestone release of the Apple Watch.

Had they said it that way, the entire live, in-person event with all its energy and fanaticism could have been reduced to a single, short email.

But it wasn't. The delivery was crucial.

As Tim Cook, CEO of *Apple*, begins his presentation, he starts with heritage. He starts by explaining how *"apple was made to make the computer more personal"*. He continues by saying, *"Over the years, we've taken this mission further than anyone could have imagined. We've created several categories of technology that have had a profound impact on peoples' lives"*. He describes the Apple retail stores as *"part of the community"* where people can *"learn and gather"*. When he announced that those stores receive 500 million visitors per year, everyone applauded. To keep this in perspective, he stated that Apple retail stores had people going to them, and people liked it.

But, because it's a journey the audience feels a part of, the achievement feels like their own.

Your answers

The journey so far has been...

....

....

....

We're proud of how far we've come together because...

....

....

....

2. The Desire

When we've been reminded of where we've come from, desire for the next stage increases:

Weddings: It's the difference between attending a wedding of strangers (*"isn't that nice"*), and a wedding of two friends whom you know have been waiting for this day to come for many years (*"they made it, finally!"*).

Sports: It's the difference between your favorite sports team winning an important game (where *"we* won") versus just any sports team winning an important game for them (where *"they* won").

Electronics: It's the difference between your preferred smartphone company releasing a new flagship device (where you presume the device is soon to be yours, before you've even seen it) and "other" smartphone companies releasing flagships of their devices.

The journey creates desire for the impending event.

Now that the journey has happened (or is happening), we have the unique opportunity to maximize that energy by creating a ceremony that celebrates where we've been, and how we've managed to get where we are now.

What we get from sharing a journey

Steve Jobs is often quoted for stating, "The journey is the reward". Let's unpack that a little:

Journeys create bias. We journey with those we trust and, since they helped choose the path, we trust the journey must be good for us, too.

Journeys create energy and excitement. Everyone longs to belong, so being present on a journey creates a sense of belonging with our travel companions. We never really want such journeys to end, do we?

Journeys create the desire to contribute. No traveler expects his companions to do all the work. Our mere presence on the journey motivates us to contribute, be it taking out the trash or live-tweeting the events.

Regardless of where it ends up, the journey itself is an opportunity to belong, to create, and to share achievement. It enables us to develop bonds with those we've come to trust, be it a journey toward a religious event, local tradition, or new smartphone release.

If you're doing important work, journeying – rather than merely transacting – with your audience could compound the reward they receive.

Example

"iPhone X has changed the industry. And along the way, it became the #1 smartphone in the world."

This is how Tim Cook introduced the iPhone Xs showreel. He continues by announcing, *"Today, we're going to take iPhone X to the next level. I'm excited to show you is by far the most advanced iPhone we have ever created".*

Apple cycled through speakers to maintain interest, then focused on product features, and demonstrated what people could do with the new product that they couldn't before. To follow it all up, they then cited that the company runs on 100% renewable energy.

The energy plans of the company received similar applause to the product itself. The audience is celebrating what they can now do (as though the product is already theirs), and how they do it (with clean energy).

This is an audience that has bought into the organization and its vision. Every win for the company feels like a win for their customers.

The new 'thing' happening at this stage of the journey is...

....

....

....

Our audience should be excited about this because...

....

....

....

3. The Future

Shared Heritage celebrates where we've been, and where we're going.

We don't celebrate a wedding for the day. We celebrate it because of where the couple has been, and what the future holds for the newlyweds.

We don't celebrate a win for our favorite sports team because of the match alone. We celebrate it because of how much work it took to get here, and what opportunities lie in the future because of this win.

Having a future together with the couple, the sports team, or an electronics company ensures we (the audience) continue to be "bought in" – that we will continue on this journey with them.

Would you celebrate the wedding if you knew they planned on getting divorced next week?

Would you continue to advocate for your sports team if you knew they were disbanding after this match?

Would you buy the flagship device if you knew there wasn't going to be another after it?

What a shared future gives us

Brendon Burchard, coach and motivational speaker, says *"the culture changed, the world changed. We moved away from a pain-oriented society into an aspirational society"*.

Aspirations exist in the future, and the future doesn't yet exist at all. With no 'reality' to hold it down, the future makes a great space for raising our ambition:

Emotional investment. A journey into the future starts in the present. If a company's version of the future sounds good, it becomes part of our own vision for the future. We want a bright future, don't we?

A vision you belong to. Because the vision is 'ours', our bias stretches beyond acceptance to advocacy. We want our own vision to come true, don't we?

Permission to raise our ambition. By advocating for that vision, its failure would mean losing the very future we hope to live in. We can't let that happen, can we?

It could be a shared future of better smartphone cameras to take better photos of your family, or it could be one where a type of crime no longer exists, so the world is safer for your children. Whatever it is, sharing a vision for the future gives us a powerful place to end a message and set the sights of our audience in the right direction.

Example

"At Apple, *we're always pushing our products forward and making technology more personal. We hope that you love these new products as much as we do.*"

This is how Tim Cook ended the iPhone Xs keynote presentation in 2018. After inviting everyone to try them out, he thanked everyone who helped make such a *magical event.*

There's an energy in the reaffirmation of the mission and direction behind the company that was well-received by the audience. It was energy in a mission the audience believes in, and a mission they feel they have the opportunity to support through their continued patronage.

There's a big difference between "I *want one of those*" and "I *want to support this*". The latter compounds the effectiveness of the former by ensuring continued commerce as an expression of a shared belief.

If the latter is what you want to achieve within your own organizations, ensure you use the *Mission Narrative* for new faces and *Shared Heritage* for your existing customers and clients.

Why our audience should feel invested in this change...

....

....

....

How the future looks for us now that this change is in place...

....

....

....

Putting it all together

This is how we journey with our tribe.

We celebrate where we've been, we celebrate where we are today, and we celebrate where we're going.

Flash sales, coupon discounts, and limited-time offers may entice people to try out your product or company, but those perks don't work on tribes without the celebration of *Shared Heritage*.

Anything less than these celebrations weakens the relationship between you and your *Person*. It makes the connection less special.

From now on, the more frequently (and more effectively) you celebrate your journey with those in your tribe, the more your organization succeeds.

This is the *Meaningful Marketing* way to create a message for those we continue to serve.

CHAPTER 5

Success Stories

Test the Methods

In this section you will find five interviews from people who have already taken the steps presented in this book.

I selected four people from vastly different industries (Arnaud, Emily, Jake, Yvonne, and Heather) and asked them all similar questions about the Meaningful Marketing steps they have taken for their businesses and about the work they have done with the process. Responses have been edited for length and clarity.

Question 1: What is your company and what does it do?

Arnaud: So, I'm an entrepreneur. I'm helping companies finding their right messaging and finding their way in the commerce sector. Also, creating other type of companies in the social environment. But that's my purpose, to help others to grow.

Emily: My company is a boutique virtual receptionist company that serves law firms across the U.S. and Canada.

Jake: My company is a company that sells unique, custom designed iPhone cases that are made with eco-friendly materials, eco-friendly packaging that have really vibrant, unique, colorful designs that really stand out when you take your phone out of your pocket. They're not like the typical drab cases that you see on most store shelves. Our company's strap-line is, *Happiness in Your Hands*. The idea is to spread a little bit of happiness in the world, a little focus on making sure that we're promoting sustainability and environmental friendliness, and enacting it in all of our actions. And the case designs really are targeted at people that may have a sense of fashionability. They're eager to find something that matches with their personality, and they just sort of show off how beautiful and colorful our world is.

Yvonne: My company started in 2013 as a response to what I saw as the death rattles of the small hospitality industry in the light of the onslaught of online travel agents and after I had in fact grown my own bed and breakfast in France beyond all expectations. What I do now is I have a process in place that helps clients to add at least 25% to their income in one season without doing more work and while having a lot more fun.

Heather: I had my own consultancy focused on helping women-owned businesses scale effectively. Now I do strategic planning, transition planning, and still help work with companies to scale effectively.

Question 2: Why is good communication important to you?

Arnaud: Well, in the end, if you have an amazing product but do not match that product with the actual audience who wants it, you definitely end up with nothing. So it's very important to have a totally coherent message across all the different touch-points with the audience you're looking for, to be able to communicate the right values, and the right value proposition. And then – all of a sudden – they magically want to buy your product!

Emily: Well, in our business, our business *is* communication. But it's also important to have a clear message, from start to finish, to attract the right clients and make sure that our messaging and our communication is always speaking to our ideal client at all times.

Jake: It's critical to be able to communicate successfully with your customer to get your message across so that you stand out in the crowd. I think the only way to be successful is if you really understand how to speak to your customer. What they're looking for, what their desires are, and how your products are a match for them. It's as much about you understanding them first before you can really communicate effectively with them, of course.

Arnaud: Unfortunately, we tend to believe that it is easier to put the cart before the horses, for some illogical reason. The last company I was in contact with believed that they'll be able to sell before they actually have a clear communication strategy and a digital strategy that makes sense. That they'll make money. What we're seeing is, when you have the right branding and communication strategy, it's a lot easier to grow from there. The end result will be a lot bigger.

Yvonne: Good communication is important because I need to be able to speak to the hearts and minds of the people that I can best help and conversely not speak to the people that I can't help. This has been a process and a journey for me because I think in any sort of consultancy role, we tend to think that we can help anybody – that we must help everybody. There are certain characteristics that I've identified about people that I can best help, where it would be most fun for me to help. It will be most profitable and fun for them, as well.

Heather: Good communication is critical, and for many reasons. One of the biggest is that when you're dealing with any target audience, I think you have to be able to connect with them in a way that they can hear you. You have to have a message that resonates with them, that gives them precisely the information that they need. So for me, a huge piece of my success has been really making sure that my messaging is clear and my story is clear.

Question 3: How has the Mission Narrative structure helped you communicate better?

Arnaud: I think what is interesting is that you have strongly structured what the wording of the core message should be, the core message of the brand, the core message of the products. It's now an easy process to fill in these forms and use those forms to figure out what the right messaging should be. And even though it's something that needs to be done with care, the end result is amazing. We saw a match very quickly with data, which is the important part because we always want to just put some fluffy words out there that might not be aligned with anything. We definitely saw time and time again the match between the right message and the right audience that was reacting very positively to it.

Emily: It is work, so I will say it was challenging at first to figure out, you know. I think, as a business owner, we get this idea of what things look like in our heads. I felt like, "Oh, I know it 100%, I know who we are and how we communicate and what we stand for". But then when you asked me to articulate it, I felt stuck and stupid. I couldn't articulate it very well, so I think going through the process of learning how to articulate your brand message and how we want to communicate as a company is a really valuable process.

Jake: It has helped me understand my customers, and the message that I'm trying to communicate to them. That's really a strong foundation. A foundation that, in some senses, was missing before going through the exercise. It wasn't something that I had even thought about, so it's really foundational to being able to communicate successfully with customers.

Yvonne: The Mission Narrative structure really got me to understand my clients' pain-points for a start, and then how to communicate the solution or the prescription that they need to resolve their problem. We went very deep into defining the problem in their language so I was able to match the language that they would know. It's almost like developing a siren call directly into the hearts and minds of the people that you can best help. So the process was very helpful to me in defining the problem and then presenting the solution in a way that they could understand and a way that I could communicate confidently. It isn't natural for us to speak in our audience's language. So, it's very useful to go through that process whereby you almost get to be in their heads.

Heather: Regarding my website, once I used the mission narrative structure, the quality of prospects improved dramatically. The number of bad prospects or people that just weren't a really good fit for me, decreased. I got less calls from them. Then people that were reaching out to me were able to because of the messaging that I had been using, because of how I had structured my story. They were often ready to buy by the time they actually reached me. They had gotten the information that they needed. So in that respect, I would say it's definitely helped. Going through this process really helped me not just to become clear on what I wanted to share with my prospects, but it also helped me to better understand their problem. So I was then able to go back and even restructure and redesign the services that I was offering a little bit so that it better fit their needs.

Question 4: What does this structure do for the audience of companies that use it?

Arnaud: From the audience standpoint, it means that they have found the holy grail, they are super happy because they've really found the brand that is talking to them and talking to their concerns or needs. So that's already an amazing first point, which leads obviously to sales, there's no question about that. From the company's standpoint, it leads to more and more engagement, and when I say more and more it's basically from a very cold first visit, it grows on and then the person is getting more and more engaged, therefore they become potentially a fan and then you've got a recurrent purchase happening super-easily. So it's using the beauty of the digital world to help a person match the company's offer to the audience needs, and magically make sales happen and create a relationship that could last many many years from then on.

Emily: It has been beneficial for our prospects as well as our audience, and it's been beneficial internally because as time has gone on, I've just become more and more committed to making sure that every piece of communication, whether it's a visual or a written communication or verbal, that everything that tells the message is always the same. I even just rolled out to my team this week some new internal brand guidelines. You don't communicate to a client if it's not in this way. The kind of thing that if someone looks at it without even reading the words, they should know that's ours.

Jake: It means that they're going to see a message that resonates with them, that will attract and appeal to them. Hopefully, they'll stick around. Hopefully, they'll decide to make a purchase, and hopefully, they'll come back, and make more purchases, and spend more time engaging with the brand.

Yvonne: It's been very interesting because what it does for my audience is it turns people on and it turns other people off, which is something that I was uncomfortable with in the beginning because, like I say, in the consultancy coaching mentoring world, we want to be able to help anybody and we don't want to upset anybody. But actually the opposite is more effective because, like I say, it sends out a siren call to the people that you can best help, but it also eliminates people that you can't help and that may cause some disruption in their pattern of behavior, for which they'll blame you. And then, you have to be very, sort of, certain about who you can help and who you can't. So, it's divisive in a good way.

And you know, at the end of the day, I'm in business because I like being in business because it's fun for me. If I'm working with clients that don't get it, they're not at a place where they can hear what I'm saying. They are not in a position in their lives where they can surrender to the process that I'm offering them that will help them to – in some cases – double their business. But if they're not in that place right now, then it's my job to identify that before they start working with me. Otherwise, it's going to be a miserable experience for me and them.

Emily: If you imagine standing on Times Square and there's this huge intersection of prospects, there's people everywhere and you just yell out, "Hey, you," you'll probably have a few heads turn. But now that we've gotten very clear on our communication and our messaging, we're saying, "Hey, Tom Smith," and only one person is turning around. So that's really what we want, we want it so defined that we know exactly who we're talking to.

Heather: They don't have to second guess and try to figure out, "Does this person really understand what I need?" It's clear. From the beginning, it's clear. "Okay, they get me, they understand the problem." They really gravitate to that confidence of you being able to say no to a client that's not a good fit. So it is a little scary but I would definitely encourage organizations to take that risk because I think they're really going to see it pay off. In my case, that confidence was actually seen by another consulting firm who was so impressed with my website and so impressed with how I had positioned myself that they ended up coming to me and offering me a position with their company, which ended up being a fabulous position working with the types of people that I wanted to work with. They mentioned multiple times that one of the reasons that I really stood out to them was the quality of my website and the quality of my messaging.

Question 5: What would you like to tell companies that haven't yet used this narrative structure?

Arnaud: Jump on it. If you already have a business, you might want to reexamine at how you can optimize – or have access to – new audiences you never thought about that could bring you the upside you're looking for in your revenue. If you are starting from scratch, it's an amazing opportunity to actually have an effortless discovery of which audiences are going to be your first and second buyers. And that is priceless. And that should be in the book of any startup that is looking to make a difference with their products.

Emily: First, prepare to do the work because in my mind, you hire a web developer or something and you tell them, "I want a website, make it beautiful", and they come back deliver you a package, but it won't articulate who is our brand. Who are we looking to speak to? Is it Tom Smith or is it Johnny Brown? Who is it? So going through this process is really important to figure out how to get what's in your head onto what's on a website and into the business and how you're going to communicate.

Jake: Give it a try. You probably have no idea what you're missing. You don't know what you don't know, and no matter how well you might think that you know the essence of your company, your brand, and your customers, it will have you thinking about all of those things in a way that you haven't before, and you're sure to uncover some valuable insights going through the process.

Yvonne: What I would say is to definitely go for it because the thing is, we think we know what people want and we think we know how they want to hear it, but actually we have no idea. And what the narrative process does is it brings out the language and the communication of the pain from your ideal client and it helps you to hone in on it. It make sure you're serving the people that you're meant to serve and not serving the people that you're not meant to serve.

Heather: I would say that going through the process is not going to just be good for marketing, but it's also really good for your business. Like I said before, it's really good for building confidence in your services, and seeing clearly how they're benefiting the world. And I think that most companies and organizations won't go through a process like this, so from a competitive advantage that's huge for you. It really gives you a competitive edge and allows you to stand out from the noise and from a higher level perspective. It really allows you to reach the people that most need and want your services or your products. So for that reason, I think if you looked at nothing else, just the fact that you'll be able to have a greater impact, I would highly recommend the process.

CHAPTER 6

What will you do about it?

Our best is our best guess

Your *Attract Your Best Customers* and *Master Your Message* sections are all full.

You've given it your best shot. I applaud you for that. You're already much closer to the result you want to see on behalf of your organization and closer to the meaningful work you'd like to continue to put out into the world.

These insights apply to your website, your email marketing, one-on-one emails, online advertising, and the way you develop your work from now on.

There are going to be many temptations to change the direction of your work, to add more bits to your message, to take bits away, or add more people alongside your *Person.*

Resist them. You know now, with the clarity and heart of a *Meaningful Marketing* strategy, that you're able to outperform, out-think and out-serve any "killer marketing hack" that may try to break your focus.

But our best it's still our best guess. Next, we need to refine our work by digging deeper and testing it out.

In defense of 'evolutionary'

'Evolutionary' is often seen as the lesser twin of 'Revolutionary'.

Evolutionary means progress. Revolutionary happens in stark contrast to the market. Some changes may be better, others may not be. Change too many things at once and you won't know which is which.

Evolutionary means survival. Revolutionary thrives on creating a lot of buzz. Buzz causes big valuations and sudden scale. But buzz doesn't stick around. All that scaling needs supporting even once valuations drop.

Evolutionary means statistical inevitability.
Revolutionary bets it all on red. Evolutionary plays enough smaller bets that it's statistically more likely to succeed, eventually.

Now we have our *Person* and our *Message*, we can allow our understanding to evolve and iterate over time.

Ironically, this is the most effective way to create something that's truly revolutionary.

Share with the team, no new tricks

'Marketing' used to be a role in a company. However, *Meaningful Marketing* isn't a role:

- Educating a prospect includes *Meaningful Marketing*.
- Educating a client includes *Meaningful Marketing*.
- Helping them evaluate includes *Meaningful Marketing*.
- User on-boarding includes *Meaningful Marketing*.
- Production includes *Meaningful Marketing*.
- Delivery includes *Meaningful Marketing*.
- Support includes Meaningful Marketing.
- Enrolling them with the best fit for their needs includes *Meaningful Marketing*.

"*Meaningful Marketing*", when done right, permeates the company with your *Person* and your *Message*.

The entire team is responsible.

It's not *a* role. It's *every* role.

Empathy is your Research and Development department

Every time you write a word or share an image with a prospect or customer, *Meaningful Marketing* will make an appearance.

How deep can empathy run in your organization?

"We made you this." What if your product ideas were born out of an understanding of your *Person's* challenges, and a willingness to solve them?

"We changed this because of what you said." What if your work developed not based on what everyone else is doing, but on what your audience needs from you?

Your *Person & Message* can become your *Research & Development*, and your work becomes a natural expression of a continuous conversation between you and your audience and shows your heart for service.

Different conversations with prospects

What do you focus on when going into sales calls?

Making a 'sale', or making a 'give'?

Making a sale: Measured in dollars up-front; they happen or they don't. Convincing someone to buy right away, regardless of whether it's a good fit or the right time for them. This is the way we were all taught to do it.

Making a give: Measured in value given up-front; it's either given or it's not. Understanding them and offering to solve real problems right away, regardless of whether or not they'll buy something. This is the new way.

Ironically, the more we focus on the latter, the more we tend to get the former anyway. The same can't be said about the reverse.

New conversations with old clients

What is a "Market Hypocrite"?

It's sadly much of the market: teams that make promises they're not equipped to keep. They know it, but are unlikely to admit it, even to themselves:

We don't trust obese dietitians: They're unlikely to have the answers, but they will often promise they do.

We don't trust broke marketers: They may compromise their genius by selling falsehoods.

We don't trust counselors on wife #6: They don't have a good record of reconciliation.

Now that we're implementing Meaningful Marketing into our companies, we have a responsibility to those who trust us to bring the whole experience to them, first.

Let's make sure there are no corners of your company that risk you becoming a "Market Hypocrite".

Commit to the Message

We don't hear much about 'Patience' and 'Focus' in business books these days.

Ironic, since missing either is catastrophic:

Patience without focus = waste. This is the long road to knowing everything and doing nothing.

Focus without patience = churn. This is the short road to pushing away everybody trying to help you.

Patience plus focus = momentum. This is the long road to making a difference.

'Hustle' and 'Hacks' sell more books than 'Patience' and 'Focus' do. But don't let that scare you or convince you to change your tactics.

Commit to your *Message*. Commit to the patience and focus it deserves.

Talk to an ImpactCoach

As a meaningful company, you're held to a higher standard. And as someone who serves meaningful companies, it's my job to hold you to that higher standard.

At this point, I will connect you with an ImpactCoach so they can look through your answers with you, live and one-on-one, to make sure that you're getting everything that you can possibly get out of this process.

It's free. Go here to find your ImpactCoach: fairhead.net/miay

'ImpactCoaching' is a program that one of our teams established to help coach people through the process of defining their *Person* and their *Message*.

This program also helps ensure that your foundations, such as the effectiveness of any writing, refining, optimizing, or expressing of your *Message*, are solid compounds.

Your ImpactCoach will make sure you haven't left anything on the table. That your offer isn't weaker than it could be. That you haven't misdiagnosed your *Person*. That you haven't under-articulated their promises and dreams. That you've fully captured the essence of the mission behind your organization.

It's free because they have optional paid continuation for those who want to go deeper. In true *Meaningful Marketing* form, the ImpactCoaching team recognizes that the best way to help people... is to help them.

People like to help

Do you struggle asking people for help?

Many people do. But the greats don't:

Newton formulated the Law of Gravity, but he wouldn't have been able to without the help of Galileo's work.

Galileo proved Heliocentrism, but he wouldn't have been able to without the help of Copernicus' theory.

Copernicus gave Galileo a theory to prove, but he needed Ptolemy's Geocentrist theories to build upon.

And so it goes on, a chain-reaction of people helping people to create breakthroughs throughout history.

If you want to optimize your Person and your Narrative work, contact your new ImpactCoach at *fairhead.net/miay*. Ask for help. It's paid for.

And help works. History proves it.

Peel back the feedback

Here are three pieces of feedback our Creative team received in the same day:

"You guys know me better than I know myself": was said by a client using one of our ImpactCoaching team's sessions. The takeaway: the session is strong, so connect more people to it.

"Your team's work was what won me this job": was said by a prospect using our Creative team's freebies. The takeaway: the freebies are strong, so connect more people to it.

"I had no idea you guys could do that": was said by a prospect of one of our Creative team's products. The takeaway: the marketing for that particular product is weak in scope awareness, address this before advertising it.

When we peel back the feedback, we usually find clues about what needs our focus.

As you test your *Person* and *Message* in the real world, you're going to see all sorts of feedback come your way. Peel it back.

Start with success

Success is not a goal.

If success is your goal, you'll be unlikely to achieve it.

I'd like to argue that "success" is a starting point, not a finishing line. An ingredient, not a destination.

Success: Trying until you reach a goal in the short/medium/long term. Unwaveringly, with commitment.

Failure: Stopping that trying process prior to goal attainment. Giving up and going home.

If you try and then achieve the goal, that's success. If you try, then stop trying, that's failure. If you try, realize it's unviable, change course, then achieve the goal, that's success. If you try, realize it's unviable, then stop trying, that's failure.

This applies to your *Meaningful Marketing*. As your *Person* changes, so does your *Message*. As you learn more about your *Person*, you learn more about your *Message* and how to adapt it.

If you've committed to maintaining a *Person* and a *Message* that use the *Meaningful Marketing* approach, you're already a success.

Now it's your turn

You have two choices.

Option 1: You take the momentum of reading this book and implement what you've learned before you forget what it said, or before you lose the inspiration or motivation to do so.

Option 2: You put it on your bookshelf and carry on doing what you were always doing, the way you've always done it, without creating new growth in your company.

If you choose Option 2, best of luck to you. Please do not take the ImpactCoaching session we've given you, because you'll only be wasting your time and theirs.

If you choose Option 1, I'm so glad we've connected. I look forward to hearing about your work, your progress, your setbacks, and your successes. Our teams collaborate actively together, and I love hearing about people like you who are brave enough to apply *Meaningful Marketing* to their companies.

Remember to get your *Toolkit* (your access code is on the back page so it's easy to find) so that we can lavish upon you as many insights, resources and examples as needed to take you to the next level.

Truly, I applaud you for what you are doing.

And I applaud you for taking the responsibility for the impact that you want to make, and for being a difference maker.

Now go.

Make a difference.

Toolkit

fairhead.net/miay

Access code:

MEANING18

Once you enter that code into the web page, you'll be given access to the email form to get the toolkit. Since the toolkit will be updated periodically, we use email to manage access so that we can provide you with the latest updates and additions.

Included will be all related resources, plus new exercises, techniques, strategies, tactics, examples, toolkits, cheat sheets, videos and PDFs, all focused on helping you communicate as effectively, empathically and viscerally as possible with your *Person*.

Also included is your accountability program, to help you take action on all of the resources in this book.